MONEY
SAVING
ideas

MONEY
SAVING
ideas

Claire Horrocks

authorHOUSE®

AuthorHouse™ UK
1663 Liberty Drive
Bloomington, IN 47403 USA
www.authorhouse.co.uk
Phone: 0800.197.4150

Published by AuthorHouse 10/30/2015

ISBN: 978-1-4969-9987-0 (sc)
ISBN: 978-1-4969-9988-7 (e)

Print information available on the last page.

Any people depicted in stock imagery provided by Thinkstock are models,
and such images are being used for illustrative purposes only.
Certain stock imagery © Thinkstock.

This book is printed on acid-free paper.

Because of the dynamic nature of the Internet, any web addresses or links
contained in this book may have changed since publication and may no longer
be valid. The views expressed in this work are those of the author and those
that completed questionnaires and do not necessarily reflect the views of the
publisher, and the publisher hereby disclaims any responsibility for them.

Scripture quotations marked NIV are taken from the Holy Bible, New
International Version®. NIV®. Copyright © 1973, 1978, 1984 by
International Bible Society. Used by permission of <u>Zondervan</u>. All rights
reserved. [<u>Biblica</u>]

Scripture quotations marked AMP are from The Amplified Bible, Old
Testament copyright © 1965, 1987 by the Zondervan Corporation. The
Amplified Bible, New Testament copyright © 1954, 1958, 1987 by The
Lockman Foundation. Used by permission. All rights reserved.

Contents

Introduction

Some time ago I began to speak to the Lord about the issue of saving money. I was sure that my money should be stretching further than it was, yet I was honouring the Lord with my finances, so it was with an element of frustration that I began to seek the Lord about this issue. I believe that the Lord told me that the people in my church do things in such a way that they are able to cut back on expenses, and so save money in different areas of their lives, and so, if we pooled these ideas we could learn from each other and save money. Praise the Lord! It is right that we become wise stewards of the money God has entrusted to us.

I presented this idea to the church, and asked them to complete a questionnaire telling them that I would put the findings into a small booklet.

Consequently, this booklet is the end result! I wish to thank those people from Bangor Assemblies of God Church, North Wales who supported this idea, and took the time to complete the questionnaire; each one is very much appreciated!

I would also like to thank Christians Against Poverty for their support and cooperation with the chapter on Debt.

I also thank others that have contributed ideas or helped in some way. I pray that those that have contributed to this will reap the rewards of their efforts, as they have sown their ideas they will reap other ideas too!

To all readers, if you benefit from just one idea in this booklet that for example saves you £5 per month, it would be £60 per year, then I consider that the idea behind this has succeeded! I believe we would all appreciate saving more and wasting less, no matter how small the amount!

As this booklet is the result of shared ideas by many people, some of the ideas included are not necessarily my own views or practise, but those that others have found beneficial to them. Some of the ideas may not be new to you, however I believe that there will be ideas here which you may not have thought of before and can use.

This booklet merely gives the reader suggestions. I cannot take responsibility for any project/idea/business agreement/ purchase that does not turn out the way that individuals hoped for.

I pray that this booklet will be of benefit to all readers, and each reader will save some money, and as a result more money will be sown into the kingdom of God.

Prosperity

Claire Horrocks

Jeremiah 29:11 NIV

"For I know the plans I have for you"
declares the Lord, "plans to prosper you
and not to harm you, plans to give you
hope and a future........

Here we see that the Lord declares Himself that He has good plans for our lives! He really is on our side! He truly is a loving heavenly Father that wants to bless His children. When a good human father delights to give good things to his children why is it that so many Christians do not believe this of their heavenly Father? This concept that God wants to prosper us is rejected by so many people that profess to be believers. Let's just look at a few definitions here:

Prosper: to thrive, do well, or be successful.

Prosperity: the condition of prospering; success or wealth.

Poverty: the condition of being without adequate food or money, scarcity, inferior quality or inadequacy.

Definitions from the Collins pocket dictionary. (Reprint 1989 edition, ISBN 0 00 433001 3)

It would make no sense to split a definition and accept that God wants us to be successful yet not be wealthy. Often the two go hand in hand, and so the same can be said of failure and to be unsuccessful can lead to poverty. The basis for our beliefs and theology must always be rooted in the Bible first, even though there are several arguments and lines of reasoning that God wants to prosper us outside of the scripture.

Deuteronomy 28:1-14 NIV

> If you fully obey the Lord your God and carefully follow all his commandments that I give you today, the Lord your God will set you high above all the nations on earth. All these blessings will come upon you and accompany you if you obey the Lord your God:
>
> You will be blessed in the city and blessed in the country.
>
> The fruit of your womb will be blessed, and the crops of your land and the young of your livestock- the calves of your herds and the lambs of your flocks.
>
> Your basket and your kneading trough will be blessed.
>
> You will be blessed when you come in and blessed when you go out.

The Lord will grant that the enemies who rise up against you will be defeated before you. They will come at you from one direction but flee from you in seven.

The Lord will send a blessing on your barns and on everything you put your hand to. The Lord your God will bless you in the land he is giving you.

The Lord will establish you as his holy people, as he promised you on oath, if you keep the commands of the Lord your God and walk in his ways. Then all the peoples on earth will see that you are called by the name of the Lord, and they will fear you. The Lord will grant you abundant prosperity – in the fruit of your womb, the young of your livestock and the crops of your ground – in the land he swore to your forefathers to give you.

The Lord will open the heavens, the storehouse of his bounty, to send rain on your land in season and to bless all the work of your hands. You will lend to many nations but will borrow from none. The Lord will make you the

> head not the tail. If you pay attention
> to the commands of the Lord your God
> that I give you this day and carefully
> follow them, you will always be at the
> top, never at the bottom. Do not turn
> aside from any of the commands I give
> you today, to the right or to the left,
> following other gods and serving them.

Here it tells us very clearly that if we live in obedience to God, then we can expect His blessing in our lives. Verse 11 says:

> The Lord will grant you abundant
> prosperity-in the fruit of your womb,
> the young of your livestock and the
> crops of your ground in the land he
> swore to your forefathers to give you.

This makes clear reference to their source of income, as well as in having families.

Verse 12

> The Lord will open the heavens, the
> storehouse of His bounty, to send rain
> on your land in season and to bless all
> the work of your hands. You will lend
> to many nations but will borrow from
> none. The Lord will make you the head,

not the tail. If you pay attention to the commands of the Lord your God that I give you this day and carefully follow them, you will always be at the top, never at the bottom.

The Lord wants to bless all of our work; He wants us to get to a place of position or authority. We are to be the head not the tail; these are positions that earn a greater income. If God does not want to prosper us financially He would not have said all that He did on the subject of working and so consequently earning money. If we are to borrow from none we need to have a good income! In fact more than good; an "abundance" is needed! God wants Christians in top positions and jobs. Imagine the impact on our nation if we have Godly people in top jobs where they can influence the lives of many e.g. the Prime Minister, government officials, M.P.s and A.M.s, those working in the media that influence what goes out on the television etc. and Christian teachers; all can have a big impact on future generations. The list could be endless. Imagine on a local level the impact in our communities with a Godly local council, doctors and nurses and scientists that could save lives simply by having God inspired ideas or pursuing a word of knowledge from God that could be ground breaking in the field of medicine. Different people find cures for all sorts of things; why shouldn't it be a Christian? Can you imagine a scientist that is a Christian finding a cure for A.I.D.S.? If we cannot imagine these things we can be almost certain that we will not see these things come to pass. We need to match our thinking with God's and dream bigger than we have allowed ourselves to do so far!

Several years ago I made a trip to Tanzania, Africa, and this was the first time I saw real poverty first hand. I don't believe that in the U.K. we see poverty on the same level as third world countries. Our benefits system in the main prevents people from experiencing true poverty. Some Christians think that to live in poverty is a spiritual place to be; I would suggest that it could instead cause people to question the love of God! True poverty causes hunger, malnutrition, stress, suicide and family break ups. It causes children in some countries to be sold into sex industries, children can become abandoned on the streets and have to fend for themselves because their parents can't feed them; this is not my idea of spirituality! My visit to Tanzania also showed me the reality of "if you don't work, you don't eat," I saw women working in the fields pregnant or with a baby strapped to their back while they did physically demanding work. I saw people's homes that I found shocking to think that people might live in them. People were begging and actually lying in the middle of a busy road as we left the airport at Dar es Salaam, risking their lives for a few coins. Poverty literally has people living in the gutter; Jesus came to restore to us all that we have lost, not to add to our losses. The Lord truly wants to prosper each of us.

Scripture Matthew 11:1-5 NIV

> After Jesus had finished instructing his twelve disciples, he went on from there to teach and preach in the towns of Galilee.
>
> When John heard in prison what Christ was doing, he sent his disciples to ask him, "Are you the one who was to come, or should we expect someone else?"
>
> Jesus replied, "Go back and report to John what you hear and see: The blind receive sight, the lame walk, those who have leprosy are cured, the deaf hear, the dead are raised, and the good news is preached to the poor.

Here Jesus sends a message to John in answer to the question "Are you the Messiah?"

His response is: ".... the blind see, the lame walk, lepers are cleansed, the deaf hear, the dead are raised up and the poor have good news!" Hallelujah! He is saying He came to meet our needs whatever they are! He wasn't simply saying that He only came to help the blind, lame, lepers, deaf etc; He was saying if you have a need I can meet that need! The good news really is good news! We have every reason to rejoice in our saviour Jesus Christ!

The "Good News" to each person is that whatever our needs, Jesus came to meet them. A blind man needs to see, a deaf person needs to hear, the lame need to walk etc. The principle here is that whatever your need is, Jesus came to meet that need! Hallelujah! A poor man needs to come out of poverty; part of the good news is that he can be prosperous!

The scripture where we see that Jesus turns the water into wine at a wedding is significant. It was the first miracle that Jesus did and He provided wine at the wedding so that the host would not be embarrassed. Jesus really cares about all areas of our lives; He cares about the things that concern us. Not only that, Jesus provided the best wine and the guests made comment because normally the best would be given first and then they would bring out a cheaper and poorer quality of wine later when nobody would notice. But Jesus made a superior quality of wine in the miracle! Jesus really does give us good gifts; He wants to give us the best and not the dregs! When we truly love someone we want to give them good gifts that have cost us something significant, we want to bless that person. And that is God's heart towards us, He wants to bless us abundantly! The question is, are we willing to receive? Or are we hung up on money and gifts and refuse to accept all that Jesus wants to give to us?

It really is a selfish mindset when someone thinks, "Well, I'm all right thank you very much, I don't need anything else," because your neighbour may need something and you may be the channel through which God wants to bless them and show them His love, and we can't give what we haven't got!

I remember years ago hearing from a young couple in my church that shared a testimony with me of how God drew them to Himself in this way.

They were living together next door to an older Christian couple. The young couple were drug addicts and they sold most of their possessions to get drugs. They were sleeping on the floor because they sold their bed to feed their habits. When the Christian neighbours heard of this they gave the couple a double bed. The young couple had never come across this before; they were shocked to say the least! But more than that, they were actually suspicious of them because the gift was so great to this needy couple! When they realised there was no 'catch' and that it was a genuine gift given because they cared about them, it brought the barriers down, not only towards the Christian couple but to God. The young couple gave their hearts to the Lord and were delivered of their addictions! Hallelujah!

If we prosper financially we have more to give to others. Let's allow God to use what He has given us, for His purposes.

We need to have our sights set on eternity, and it takes money to get the gospel to a lost world; let's not get hung up on money issues. Imagine having a pay rise in your job, or an income if you are unemployed; then you would be in a position to support charities, ministries, missionaries, maybe do a trip yourself where you can actively serve God. It is common sense that the more money we earn then we can sow more into the kingdom of God. If earthly fathers delight in giving gifts to their children then how much more does a good God delight in blessing His children? I now find that I am blessed when I give, it makes me feel really happy when I give a gift to someone. We are made in God's image, so surely that is how God feels when we receive His gifts. And He delights when we are blessed!

Mark 6:32-44 NIV

So they went away by themselves in a boat to a solitary place. But many who saw them leaving recognised them and ran on foot from all the towns and got there ahead of them. When Jesus landed and saw a large crowd, he had compassion on them, because they were like sheep without a shepherd. So, he began teaching them many things.

By this time it was so late in the day, so his disciples came to him. "This is a remote place" they said, "and it's already very late. Send the people away so that they can go to the surrounding countryside and villages and buy themselves something to eat."

But he answered, "You give them something to eat."

They said to him, "That would take eight months of a man's wages!" Are we to go and spend that much on bread and give it to them to eat?"

"How many loaves do you have?" he asked. "Go and see."

When they found out, they said, "Five — and two fish."

Then Jesus directed them to have all the people sit down in groups on the green grass. So they sat down in groups of hundreds and fifties. Taking the five loaves and the two fish and looking up to heaven, he gave thanks and broke the loaves. Then he gave them to the disciples to set before the people. He also divided the two fish among them all. They all ate and were satisfied,

and the disciples picked up twelve
basketfuls of broken pieces of bread
and fish. The number of men who had
eaten was five thousand.

The feeding of the 5000 teaches us how our little can become much in the hands of Jesus! Whoever gave the five loaves and two fishes gave up their lunch that day. But the scriptures tell us that 5000 received their lunch after Jesus had blessed it, because of what that individual gave to the Lord. Not only that, there were 12 baskets full of leftovers so everyone had their fill, nobody went hungry. God wants us to have enough so that we can give on every occasion!

2 Corinthians 9:11 NIV

You will be made rich in every
way so that you can be generous on
every occasion, and through us your
generosity will result in thanks-
giving to God.

That person would have seen their offering not only come back to them but also multiplied many, many times over, and right before their eyes! They effectively sowed their lunch and got their lunch back and saw an amazing miracle take place! Jesus must have delighted to do this for him. What a message that person received that day. Whatever we give to the Lord, He can bless, multiply and use it to bring a blessing to others. Had he had a poverty mentality I doubt very much that he would have shared his lunch. He would have been too fearful to share it in case he didn't eat again that day, but he put the needs of others before his own and he received back in abundance!

If we want to prosper we must put the Lord first in our lives and honour Him with all that we have; a key to this is to be obedient in the area of tithing!

Tithe

The tithe is where we give 10% of our income to God; alternatively we can view this quite differently and see the tithe as God letting us keep 90% of our income! The point being that all we have actually belongs to God not us, as we are stewards of what He has sent our way. This is a very helpful and sobering point of view on the whole subject of the tithe.

For us as Christians, we need to view the tithe as a requirement of God and not an optional extra. The bible talks about tithing in the Old Testament; it is first mentioned in:

Leviticus 27:30 Amplified

> And all the tithe of the land, whether of the seed of the land or of the fruit of the tree, is the Lord's; it is holy to the Lord.

Here we see that the tithe belongs to the Lord not us.

Malachi 3:10 Amplified

> Bring all the tithes (the whole tenth of your income) into the storehouse, that there may be food in My house, and prove Me now by it, says the Lord of hosts, if I will not open the windows of heaven for you and pour you out a

blessing, that there shall not be room enough to receive it.

Here we see that the tithe is actually a tenth of our income, so by whatever means we earn an income we need to commit to giving the Lord the first 10% of that, no matter how big or small that amount is. This shows the justice of the God that we serve, because no matter what we earn God requires the first tenth, not because He is short of money, He isn't. This isn't really about money but it is a matter of the heart; my heart and yours! Where we spend our money shows us and God where our heart really lies. By giving the Lord the first 10% we are showing God that we are honouring Him with our income and putting Him first in our lives. We make sure that we give to Him first because if we don't we can almost certainly guarantee that there will not be any money left at the end of the month, in which to pay the tithe.

Money is such an issue in today's society and can so easily have a hold of us. But then that also happened in biblical times. Jesus challenged a rich young ruler about where his heart really lay.

Luke 18:18-30 NIV

A certain ruler asked him, "Good teacher, what must I do in order to inherit eternal life?"

"Why do you call me good?" Jesus answered "No-one is good-except God alone. You know the commandments: "Do not commit adultery, do not murder, do not steal, do not give false testimony, honour your father and mother."

"All these I have kept since I was a boy" he said.

When Jesus heard this he said to him, "You still lack one thing. Sell everything you have and give it to the poor, and you will have treasure in heaven. Then come, follow me."

When he heard this, he became very sad, because he was a man of great wealth. Jesus looked at him and said "How hard it is for the rich to enter the kingdom of God! Indeed, it is easier for a camel to go through the eye of a needle than for a rich man to enter the kingdom of God."

Those who heard this asked, "Who then can be saved?"

Jesus replied "What is impossible with men is possible with God."

Peter said to him "We have left all we had to follow you!"

"I tell you the truth" Jesus said to them, "no-one who has left home or wife or brothers or parents or children for the sake of the kingdom of God will fail to receive many times as much in this age and, in the age to come, eternal life."

The fact that Jesus tells him to sell everything and then follow Him suggests several things about this man. Firstly, up until that point he wasn't born again or Jesus wouldn't have told the ruler to follow Him, if he already was! Secondly, the commandments that he had kept suggest that he was morally a good man or maybe religious and he was trying to please God as much as his understanding allowed him.

In Mark 10:21 we gain more insight into this meeting:

Jesus looked at him and <u>loved him</u> "One thing you lack" he said "Go, sell everything........ (NIV)

It's important to put the words that Jesus said to him into the context of the fact that Jesus loved him! Jesus knew this young man's heart, and He knew that his wealth mattered greatly to him, and the young ruler went away sad when Jesus told him to part with his possessions. The fact that he had great wealth wasn't a problem to Jesus; it was the place that his wealth had in his life that was the problem. Jesus effectively asked him to put it on the altar so that his heart would truly belong to Him. The Lord wants to be first in our lives, and if we are to live effectively for Him we need to ensure that we place on the altar the things that would take His rightful place in our lives.

The subject of the tithe challenges many; are we really living for Him because we say we are, or do our actions show us and God where our heart lies? If we love God we will obey Him, see John 14:23 NIV

> Jesus replied "If anyone loves me, he will obey my teaching. My Father will love him, and we will come to him and make our home with him. He who does not love me will not obey my teaching. These words you hear are not my own; they belong to the Father who sent me."

If the rich young ruler had done as Jesus said, I believe that, because of the principal of sowing and reaping, he would have received back what he gave away with interest! Jesus actually loved him and was showing him what he needed to do to come into a relationship with God. Jesus had eternity in mind. I have sometimes wondered whether or not this young man did give his heart to Jesus some time later.

God is for us and not against us. He really wants to bless us in our lives just like any good earthly father wishes to do with his children. Many see God as an ogre that is just waiting to catch us out in sin so that He can beat us up! No matter what our own human father was like with us or is still with us now, let's choose to base our view of God from a biblical viewpoint and not from any negative experiences we may have had with our own human father. The tithe is not an opportunity for God to deprive us of things but in fact the opposite is true.

Giving the tithe causes us to link up with God and to receive His blessing. As we honour Him we set ourselves into position to have our needs met by the Lord.

Luke 6:38 NIV

> *"Give, and it will be given to you. A good measure, pressed down, shaken together and running over will be poured into your lap. For with the measure you use, it will be measured to you."*

I believe that when we do not give God the tithe we actually set ourselves up for lack; we need to do things God's way not the world's.

Malachi 3:10 NIV

> Bring the whole tithe into the Store-
> house, that there may be food in my
> house. Test me in this," says the Lord
> Almighty, "and see if I will not throw
> open the floodgates of heaven and pour
> out so much blessing that you will not
> have room enough for it....

Here we see that the Lord tells us to test Him in giving a tithe; He promises us such a blessing when we obey Him. I believe that it is the only thing that He encourages us to test Him in. I find this quite a surprise that He would encourage us to test Him in this! I think that this is an indication to us that to tithe isn't something that we would naturally want to do and it is an area where many Christians are not obedient. God knows that when we give Him our tithe we will be blessed, and so He encourages us to do this.

We do have to take tithing seriously. I personally didn't learn to tithe until I became a student, and this was something that I did need to repent of! I think fear of how I was going to manage financially caused me to reassess my life and I became more determined to do things God's way and not mine. At the time I had a small student grant which wasn't easy for me after I had been working for about 6 years, though I was grateful that it wasn't a loan. However, God provided so well for me during the 4 years as a student and I even came out of college without any debts! The Lord provided wonderfully for me; I had excellent digs for less than other students were paying elsewhere, I had the use of a car as well as the convenience of central digs. This really did encourage me and it is a testimony of God's faithfulness to His promise; that He would provide for all my needs.

We can always find reasons to withhold our tithe. When money is short we can so easily justify to ourselves several reasons why we should not be obedient. These are really excuses and we should not be talked into it by fear. The devil can't make us be disobedient to God once we have given our lives to Him, so he has to talk us into it. Fear is probably one of his main tools that he uses in our lives to get us to do what he wants instead of what God wants. Through fear of not being able to pay the bills, etc. we can be conned into thinking that it's sensible to withhold the tithe, and pay the bills first. This is where we are called to walk in faith and trust that our God really will meet all of our needs! Not just some of them but all of them, that is what the scripture says.

Remember, praise God you have a tithe to give! When I went to Africa many years ago I remember someone in the church put a live chicken in the offering! We all have something to give even if it is not money. Let's be determined to honour God in this. As you give your tithe, name your seed and expect to see God provide for your every need.

Claire Horrocks

Try to sow into a similar need for example, someone you know is trying to save up money for a car and you also need one; sow money into their car and name your seed as provision of a car for yourself, and expect God to provide for you! If you wanted to grow tomatoes you would need to plant tomato seeds. We get what we sow and that applies to other areas of our lives too!

Debt

If you are struggling with unmanageable debt, it's important that you remember that God is there for you no matter how bad your problems get.

1 Peter 5:7 NIV

> *Cast all your anxiety on him because he cares for you.*

1 Peter 5:7 Amplified

> *Casting the whole of your care (all your anxieties, all your worries, all your concerns, once and for all) on Him, for He cares for you affectionately and cares about you watchfully.*

You may feel overwhelmed by your problems but God isn't fazed by them. Though you don't have the answers yet, God does!

Debt

If you are struggling with unmanageable debt, and you would like to receive support and advice, I suggest that you contact Christians Against Poverty (CAP). CAP is a debt counselling charity that works in partnership with local churches across the U.K., Australia, Canada and New Zealand to provide free and comprehensive support that enables people to become debt free. CAP will help anyone regardless of their religious beliefs, race, nationality, age, gender, marital status, sexuality or disability. Clients are given the opportunity to give to the charity in order to help them assist more people, and many clients are grateful for the empowering opportunity to give back, but this is completely voluntary.

Many people have testified to the superb help and support they have received from this charity, and they have had their hope restored. To see some true stories of how people's lives have been transformed by CAP, check out www.capuk.org.

To find your nearest CAP Debt Centre, just type in your postcode at the top of the webpage, or if you would like more information about the charity and its services, call 0800 328 0006.

How CAP can help you

When you phone CAP they will connect you with a local church-based CAP Debt Coach. The Debt Coach will arrange to visit you in your own home to gather your financial information and send it to the debt counselling specialists at CAP's Head Office in Bradford. They draw up a livable budget for you to stick to, and they also liaise with your creditors in order to reduce interest rates and negotiate repayment terms. This means you will stop receiving calls and threatening letters from your creditors hounding you to repay them. Or if insolvency is the best route out of debt, CAP will support you through the entire process, attending court hearings with you and assisting with all the paperwork.

Whatever your debt solution, all you need to do is stick to your budget and make one monthly payment into your CAP Plan and CAP will do the rest. Support is available for every step of your journey, on the phone or in person, and volunteers from the local church, known as Befrienders, offer emotional support throughout.

Countless clients have testified that making that first step in contacting CAP changed, or even saved, their lives. The effects of debt on individuals and their families can be devastating; CAP has proven to be a lifeline to so many people across the world.

If you are not in debt but feel that you could handle your finances better, CAP has developed a revolutionary money management course called the CAP Money Course. To find out more information about this have a look at: www.capmoney.org

The course is built around the simple premise of Budget – Save – Spend, and covers issues such as:

- How to get your money under control.
- How to make informed and good financial decisions.

- Short and medium term financial goals.
- Maintaining control of your finances once the system is established.

CAP has also introduced CAP Job Clubs and CAP Release Groups into their services, which support members to get back into employment and to break free from life controlling dependencies, respectively. For more information on all CAP's services, check out www.capuk.org, or call 0800 328 0006.

Food

- Supermarkets are competing with one another for your custom so there are always special offers on. Make the most of 'buy one get one free' offers; you can store or sometimes freeze the extra one or give it away and bless someone else.

- When comparing food items compare the price per 100g rather than the actual prices of the item.

- Fruit and vegetables can sometimes be bought cheaper at the grocers; bargains can be found if you are planning on using your purchases quickly.

- Shop around to find goods at cheaper prices. Many items can vary in price significantly from store to store. Shop in more than one place.

- Make a list of all the things you need, and stick to it! Make the list gradually throughout the week adding to it the things you run out of. This way you have confidence in your list. If you think of something that isn't on your list, whilst you are in the store, it's possible you don't really need it!

- Plan your meals and make a menu for the week, then make your list according to what you really need. This is particularly helpful if you live on your own as it helps to prevent wastage with perishable food e.g. vegetables, salad items etc. which quickly go off.

- Make your own packed lunch and take it to work for lunch times; this is far more economical than buying ready-made sandwiches etc. or eating out.

- Fruit and vegetables can be bought more cheaply by buying in season, as imported foods can be more expensive.

- Bags of fruit sometimes can work out to be cheaper than loose fruit but you can't inspect your fruit the same when it is packed.

- Look at the supermarket pamphlets that come through your door; compare prices between the supermarkets as they can vary. If you do see bargains you want to buy, try to get to the store quickly because these items in the pamphlets can soon sell out. Also be aware that these are designed to get you into the store to spend money, so if you are going in for just one or a few items be disciplined and only buy what you went in for!

- Where you read 'maximum 3 items per customer' these can represent really good value for money.

- Where items are reduced substantially consider buying twice or three times what you need, if it's something that you can keep and use in time, make the most of it while the offer is on!

- If you live in shared accommodation you can cut your food bill by pooling your food money, and getting all your food items from that shared kitty. Sharing the making of the list and doing the shopping can also save time and effort. Keeping this money in a shared kitty means that when you run out of something you can buy what you need taking the money from there. Alternatively just simply sharing the staple foods e.g. butter, milk, etc. can also be helpful.

- Pre-packed fruit and vegetables can be more expensive, so weigh them and buy them loose. Weighing food is a good idea so that you know how much it will cost before you get to the till! This helps you to keep more careful control of your spending.

- Items like specially prepared jacket potatoes can be particularly expensive, when they can be easily bought and prepared quickly anyway at a fraction of the cost.

- Try not to do your food shopping at meal times or if you are hungry; it's surprising what you may be tempted to buy when you are hungry, things that you don't really need. Some of us are more likely to buy junk food at times like this!

- Stews and soups are full of nutrients and can be very economical to make yourself. Also home made vegetable soup is low in calories which is an added bonus! Liquidize those for children that don't like vegetables. Pasta dishes with sauces, marmalades/

chutneys can be economical to make; give these away as gifts too.

- Most of the supermarkets do their own brands. These are always cheaper than the famous makes; however, be selective as some are cheaper by far but not necessarily as enjoyable to eat.

- Get into the habit of paying for all your food by cash. It helps to use cash for other purchases as well because using cash instead of a debit or credit card really brings home the amount that we have spent. It also pulls us up as we go around a supermarket not to get tempted into buying things that we haven't planned or budgeted for. Be careful though not to get caught out at the till without enough money to pay for all the items! This could be very embarrassing and it could take a while to sort this out with the cashier!

- Consider the use of a store loyalty card; the points collected are rewarded with money off tokens etc. Ask your friends/family about different stores because you can think that you are getting a good deal when there may be a better one to be had elsewhere. This happened to me, and I changed where I bought my diesel and got it from the same place as my weekly shopping. This gave me far more points and I noticed a difference very quickly and I received more back at a quicker rate. I think we sometimes get a good deal initially which draws us in, and then the deal isn't so good for us after a while, and we simply don't notice or just get used to going to the same place.

- Cooking for one can be done more economically by using a pan that has steaming containers on the top. A meal can be cooked on one ring instead of using 2 or 3, and so save on fuel as well. The containers can be used for steaming vegetables, or fish wrapped in foil whilst potatoes or other vegetables are boiling in the pan below. If you put the vegetables in towards the end of the cooking time, they retain more nutrients, stay a better colour as well as staying firmer.

- Go shopping with a friend to a supermarket and look for the offers where it's cheaper to buy 2 or 3 in one go and afterwards share these items and you will both save money.

- Buying in bulk is not always a money saver; some items like fruit and vegetables go off if not eaten quickly, so you can end up throwing food out and wasting money!

- Buy carrots in bulk and blanch cook them. Then pack into bags according to servings and freeze them. These are ready for use when required.

- Visit www.mysupermarket.co.uk - great for making supermarket comparisons!

Home

- When you are acquiring a home for the first time, buy some second hand furniture to help you out initially. These can be gradually replaced with new items as you save money.

- Wait for the sales and save, particularly when buying bigger items.

- If you live alone, or you are a married couple or small family, having a water meter fitted can help you to save money depending on how much water is used. These are usually fitted free but remember these often cannot be removed once installed, so it's worth considering if you think you may want to sell your house in the future. Having a meter fitted could possibly narrow down the number of potential buyers, should you wish to sell the property in the future.

- Use better quality products e.g. washing up liquid, as they last longer than cheaper ones.

- Use energy saving light bulbs.

- Switch off unnecessary things when not in use; don't leave the television on standby. Don't forget to keep your fridge freezer on though!

- I knew someone that bought a flat and was starting almost completely from scratch regarding the furniture. She made the most of the sales and bought all the major big things she needed from a few stores with her credit card in a short space of time. She also arranged for the items to be delivered by the various stores on the same day so that she only had to use one day of her holiday entitlement. She then did a lot of overtime at work until the bill was completely paid off. This worked for her because she knew she could definitely work the extra hours each week, and the need to do so was only a short term measure not a long term or permanent one. She also managed to pay off the debt without having to pay too much interest because she paid it off quite quickly.

Clothes

- Look for clothes in the sales which you may be able to buy and use at a different time e.g. buy summer clothes in the end of season sale ready for the next summer. This can be risky if it's not the fashion you still want the next season but some items are a standard design so this could be beneficial.
- Buy good quality clothes which may be more expensive initially but last longer.
- You can get pounds off items by opening a store card when you make a purchase. This can be a great saving when spending a large amount, because the more you spend the greater the saving if they have a promotional offer on at the time. Just because you open a store card account doesn't mean that you are promising to shop there again, although the store is hoping that this will happen. Just remember to budget for this when the bill comes through, so that you can make the minimum payment required and hopefully you don't incur charges. It is preferable to pay the full amount off in the first payment, so that you don't end up having to pay for the privilege of credit on top of the existing bill. Be aware that store cards can be very costly to use if you don't pay for items when the bill comes. If you know that you won't be able to pay up straight away then question whether you should buy the item.

- Save money each month specifically for clothes and be determined not to dip into this designated money for anything else.

- Bargains can be found in supermarkets and various charity shops. Some clothes in charity shops have never been worn and sometimes still have the shop tag on them. Shopping outlets can be good for quality products and designer labels at low prices.

- Buy clothes abroad when on holiday, these can prove to be really cheap and also you can make unusual purchases that will be more unique.

- Give quality clothes away, sow and you will reap. Charity shops will gladly receive good quality clothes that are clean and didn't come out of the Ark!

- Children's clothes can be bought in charity shops and this can save you a lot of money when you consider how quickly children grow and soon their clothes no longer fit them. This is good especially for their outdoor play clothes, which do get ruined quickly anyway.

- Question whether designer clothes are really necessary for children.

- Carefully choose your basic items as they will probably be worn more often. Think also how you can mix and match and get the most out of your clothes.

- Make sure you know which colours suit you and which flatter you the most. These are not necessarily the colours that you like the best; the 'wrong' colours worn can seemingly drain colour from someone if worn next to their face. If possible pay to have a consultation with an expert in these matters. Even though they can be quite costly they can save you money in the long run, as you receive sound advice from someone who knows what they are talking about. One consultation could cost the same as one 'wrong' outfit, so it is worth considering and can be seen as an investment! You will learn about the colours and styles that suit you, and so help you to make good and wise purchases. Looking good helps us to feel more confident and helps promote good self-esteem. This would also make a wonderful gift for someone, and maybe consider asking for a beauty consultation as a birthday gift for yourself as well, if you don't have the money. Failing that, read up on the subject with these books:

- Colour me Beautiful- Carole Jackson (Published by Piatkus 1983, ISBN 0-86188-299-7)

- What Not To Wear- Trinny Woodall & Susannah Constantine (Published by Weidenfeld & Nicolson 2002, ISBN 0-297-84331-1)

In the Colour Me Beautiful book Carole Jackson helps you to define which 'season' you are, therefore which colours will compliment you. She also includes a palate of colours for you to use as a guide, and to help you match your colours correctly when shopping. As you begin to replace your wardrobe gradually, you begin to find that more of your clothes will mix and match more successfully.

In the book: What Not To Wear by Trinny and Susannah, it shows many examples of styles that either flatter different body shapes or show why some styles are simply not suited for particular body shapes. There are also television programmes that give advice on these matters.

- Keep a regular check on your weight and body shape! Putting on weight that makes our clothes uncomfortable becomes a costly thing when clothes have to be replaced. If you find that you are putting on weight and clothes are starting to feel tight, resolve in your heart to start addressing the issue of weight gain, decide on a solution and start putting this into practice.
- I have found that slimming clubs are worth the investment in order to lose weight and live a healthier lifestyle. Once you reach your goal weight you don't usually pay to attend classes. You receive support, recipes and ideas for meals, accountability and the opportunity to meet new people.

- Don't get carried away using more washing powder/conditioner than your clothes really need. Too much causes clothes to fade and so they are not so flattering to wear if they look pale and literally washed out! Also this brings an unnecessary expense to your shopping if you need to buy washing powder more regularly. Some are more highly concentrated and so designed to use less, but we can be creatures of habit and still use the original amount instead of adjusting the amount according to the instructions on the packet!

- Over-loading the washing machine can be false economy because the clothes don't get as clean as they would in a normal load, and also you risk a costly repair if the machine breaks down. Equally, be economical with the water and power supply when doing your washing and don't put on a wash that has only got a few items in.

- Leaving the machine switched on all day wastes electricity; try and make sure that you are around to switch it off when the wash has finished.

Car

- Pay for road tax for a year instead of 6 months because it is usually cheaper.
- If possible spread out the payments for the tax, MOT, insurance, service etc, throughout the year rather than paying for these all at once or at other expensive times of the year.
- Paying insurance by direct debit can be helpful for some people; however be aware of the fact that you usually end up paying more.
- Road tax can be purchased monthly by setting up direct debit with the Post Office, this helps to spread the cost!
- Smaller engines can be more economical in fuel and road tax. This is worth checking out before you buy a car!
- Keep a watch on where the cheapest fuel can be bought; loyalty to a garage doesn't always pay!
- Regular servicing can help retain the value of your car. This can also help prevent major repair work being done; however remember that servicing isn't generally cheap. Do your own checks on the water, oil and tyre pressure regularly.
- Leaving repairs that you suspect/know needs to be done is dangerous for you and for others on the road. It can cost you more in the long run when you finally get it fixed if the delay causes further damage to your car.

- If you can afford it get a new car every 3 years; you shouldn't have repair charges and often things are thrown in for free.
- Set a budget on how much you are prepared to pay weekly for your fuel and plan your usage accordingly.
- Do you need to fill the tank up to the maximum? We may run the car more economically if we don't fill it to the top.
- Question if you really need to make a particular journey or not.
- Plan your travelling so that you are not unnecessarily making the same journey twice.
- Share the cost of travelling with friends; take it in turns using each others cars.
- If you pay for insurance by direct debit, be sure to check you are onto a good deal before it automatically takes you into your next year. You usually have to stop it yourself or they assume you don't want to change. This can be a sneaky way that they tie you into a more expensive deal.
- By driving slower it reduces the drag on the car and so uses less fuel and saves wear on the tyres.
- Compare petrol/diesel prices on: petrolprices.com

Holidays

- Some foreign holidays can prove to be quite cheap because the cost of living can be low in some countries. Keep up to date with how the euro and other currencies compare.
- Visiting people you know can help cut the cost down!
- If you are not restricted by the time you go, i.e. children/school, or you can take your holidays whenever you want to, and if you don't really mind where you go, then some holiday bargains are possible if you can go at short notice, especially those outside of school holidays. There is a significant difference in the price if your holiday has to be taken during the school holidays. If you are able to plan a holiday when it doesn't overlap with such a time then you can save money!
- Camping is a cheaper way to have a holiday; there are quality campsites which offer good facilities. This can be a real option for families or people on a limited income.
- It might be possible to borrow some camping gear to try out this kind of holiday. Be sure you enjoy camping before committing yourself to the expense of buying all the gear. It can be a waste of money if you find you don't enjoy it!
- Full board can work out cheaper in the long run if that is what you want. It can also help you to budget

your spending money if you don't have to pay for an evening meal each day, but don't forget your lunch which often isn't included in the price.

- Try looking for cafés and restaurants away from the main tourist parts. They are often much cheaper than the first ones you come across and you can get more pleasant and quicker service. These also give you a truer picture of life in the region as well.

- Little things add to the cost of a holiday significantly. Look out throughout the year for bargains that you may need to take with you, e.g. sun cream. However, be sure that the expiry date hasn't run out before you use it; or you may find it doesn't offer the protection that you expect. Swimwear can be bought cheaply in the summer sales ready for the next year.

- Sometimes sun cream can be cheaper abroad, but you run the risk of not getting just what you need if you don't take it with you.

- If you are travelling by air be sure not to go over the weight allowance in your case; it can prove costly if you have to pay for the extra weight at the airport! This can also be a blow to your holiday spending money.

- Plan in advance so that you can save up specifically for your holiday without any unexpected bills. Also when you pay at the last minute you usually have to pay the full amount when you book the holiday.

- Don't forget the cost of your holiday insurance when booking your holiday. It is not worth the risk to go without adequate cover.
- Establish a touring base which has a lot to do or see around it rather than going somewhere that looks good but is the only place for miles around. It can get very expensive if you are relying on public transport just to get where there might be restaurants, site-seeing attractions etc.

Organisation and Budgeting

- Plan your meals in advance so that you only buy what you need for the week.
- Make sure you go shopping with a list; we always buy things we don't need without a list!
- Space out the buying of more expensive items that you don't need to buy each week, e.g. washing powder, tea bags, coffee etc.
- Do the same with expenses such as car tax, car insurance, MOT so that they don't all fall in the same month.
- When you get paid make sure you pay your tithe first and then put a set amount away for savings. After this adjust your spending according to what is left when all direct debits are paid.
- If you are struggling to save each month write down everything you spend and see where your money is going; this way you will see clearly if you are spending on unnecessary items or spending too much when you could be cutting back.
- When you are saving for a specific item/need put that money in a special account specifically for that and don't take from it for anything else.
- Some people find that it's worthwhile to shop on-line and pay for the supermarket to deliver your shopping to your home. This cuts out impulse buying and some people say they save money as well as time by doing this.

Christmas

- Don't be taken in by the world's influence at Christmas time! Be sensible, buy what you can afford, not what you feel pressured into. Set your limit and stick to it. Don't go into debt for Christmas and spend the rest of the year paying for it! It really is the thought that counts and not the cost of a gift. People usually appreciate the fact that you have remembered them.

- Pay for Christmas before it arrives and start to save in January! Don't burden the New Year with debts resulting from the Christmas just passed. Even a small amount put away each month will help.

- Don't be influenced into buying things you don't really want!

- Remember not to spend as though the shops were closing forever i.e. don't panic buy! Most food shops are only closed for a day!

- Make your shopping list before you hit the shops! This could help you stick to your budget and not be taken in by clever promotions.

- Be creative and use the talents God has given you! Make gifts for people as this can save you money. Home-made gifts and cards are very personal and show that you care because you have put thought, time and effort into their gift.

- Give what the recipient would like rather than what you would personally like; you may need to research this! Make a note of things your family and friends express interest or preferences in, e.g. the type of perfume/aftershave they use, gifts like these are often very personal and most people have a favourite.

- Buy Christmas cards/wrapping paper and gifts in the January sales and throughout the year. Sometimes items are more costly just before the Christmas season.

- Look out for deals like 'buy one get one free.'

- Look after your decorations so that you can use them each year.

- Add to your collection by buying a new one each year in the January sales.

- If you are happy to have an artificial tree invest in a good one so that it will last for years.

- Alternatively you could buy a real one every other year and use an artificial one in the years in between.

- At Christmas if you have a real tree then consider recycling it. Plant it in your garden if the roots are still on it. If it's in a tub with the roots then re-pot it into a bigger tub and put it outside, and use it next year with no digging required.

- Switch off the tree lights when you're not there to appreciate them, save on using the energy.

- Challenge yourself to consider if you really need all that you buy each year. Why not eat different things that might be cheaper?

- Make sure that you write your cards early enough to post them second class instead of first. Likewise any gifts that need to be posted need to be bought early enough as well. Put a reminder on your calendar giving you enough shopping time so that you don't get caught out.

- Gifts that will need to be posted need to be transportable as well as light!

- Cards that are designed specially to go abroad can be costly! Why not make a personal card made from a photograph; this could add that personal touch as well as being cheaper!

- Buy an occasional gift throughout the year so that you can spread the cost of Christmas gifts; however remember there is a limit regarding when you can return things to the shops so don't get caught out. It's usually about 28 days so only do this with gifts you are certain about! Some shops will give a 'gift receipt' for the purpose of returning an unwanted gift; be sure to ask for one, and check how long it will be valid.

Savings

- If you have a heavy purse/wallet which frequently contains excess coins, consider putting them into a piggy bank, glass jar etc. You tend not to miss a few coins but after 2 or 3 months of doing this you could be pleasantly surprised by the amount that you have saved. It would be worth the effort of counting the coins, placing them into separate money bags and depositing them at your bank.

- Try to save some money each week. Even if this is just a small amount it builds up over time and can also be used if you run short or have an emergency.

- If you pay tax an ISA can be a good saver for you, but look into this thoroughly before you commit to it.

- Save energy wherever possible in the home. Advice can be sought from the gas/electricity suppliers who will give you useful leaflets to help inform you where money might be being wasted. Make sure the loft is well insulated and your hot water tank has a jacket on or you waste money.

- Switch lights off when you leave the room, and use energy saving light bulbs anywhere you can.

- Don't leave electrical equipment on standby; turn it off because you pay for it on standby!

- If you have gas central heating, turn the heating down at the thermostat and this will reduce your gas bill. Turning down the temperature on your washing machine also saves on the electricity bill.

- Make sure the washing machine is full before you use it.

- Dry as much washing as you can outside in the fresh air. It is costly using a spin dryer especially if you can do it for nothing outside. Putting wet clothes on the radiators can be false economy if it causes you to turn the heating up!

- Compare prices with different power companies, loyalty doesn't always pay!

- Many people are putting their money into property as a buy to let. This is worth considering; if the house prices increase you can make money. Be sure to consider this very carefully though, to ensure that you can make the payments if you go for a period of time where you don't have a tenant.

- Use a separate bank/building society account to save for specific things e.g. car/maintenance, holidays, Christmas etc. Arrange for a set amount to be transferred automatically shortly after pay day each month so that you don't run the risk of forgetting or choosing to use the money elsewhere. This way you find that you already have some of the money you need when the bill comes and you don't have quite as much money to find at once.

Paying Bills

- If you have made savings by being careful with the use of electricity, gas, phone etc. remember to have your monthly payments adjusted accordingly.
- Shop around for the best deals. There is a lot of competition for your custom and so deals change regularly. Remember a good deal doesn't always remain a good deal forever, so if you keep a watch on various offers you can benefit by changing your supplier.
- Some stores operate a stamp system, so you can buy for example £5 worth of stamps and at a later date pay for items in that store using the stamps. This could help with the cost of Christmas by buying stamps each week, but keep them safe!
- Using one company for gas and electricity can save money instead of dealing with two but look into this first.

Direct Debit

Paying by direct debit has several advantages:

- You often get a better deal if you choose this method of payment.
- It prevents you forgetting to pay a particular bill and so not getting penalised for a late payment.
- It takes the stress out of remembering and it is less hassle; you don't waste time paying for different commodities.
- It also helps you to budget your money at the beginning of the month, and makes paying large bills more manageable and less painful!
- Many things can be paid for by direct debit: electricity, gas, water, television license, telephone, home/contents insurance, car insurance/recovery, health/dental insurance cover, gifts of support to various charities/ ministries etc. which could help with your monthly budget by spreading the cost.

- Keep an up to date list of all the things you pay for by direct debit and be sure to alter this as prices change. This way you won't get caught out with more going out of your bank account than you have budgeted for!

Credit Cards

- Use a store credit card and get money knocked off the price. Make sure you pay for the item in the given time so that you don't pay interest. Write the date on your calendar so that it doesn't get forgotten, and you can budget for the payment.

- Only use a credit card if you can make the payments when they start. Interest on these cards makes using them for non-essentials questionable. Remember, items bought with a credit card have to be paid for; don't be lulled into a false sense of security with them. If they are not used wisely they are a snare. They can be very useful for paying for items over the phone/internet, such as theatre tickets etc. but remember to pay for them when the credit card bill comes straight away. If you chose to pay by credit card and you know you won't be paying for it when the bill comes, then work out how much you could potentially end up paying for the item with the interest added per month. Ask yourself if you think it's really worth it. Is it really necessary to purchase it by credit card or can you wait until you have saved enough to pay for it up front?

- Some people make the decision to never use credit cards preferring instead to save up for the item and then buy it.

Insurance

- Many stores try to get you to buy insurance for the item you have bought, whilst you are at the till paying for it. Try and consider this before paying for the item because some people can easily feel under pressure and buy something that they don't really want. Some of these insurances might be worth considering. However some items are so cheap that it would be more economical to buy a replacement item than to pay the insurance premiums.

- Some insurance companies encourage customers to pay their premiums by direct debit. When you do this they usually write to you a short time before the renewal date is due, to inform you that you don't need to change anything, and the current arrangement will continue for another year unless you cancel it. If you don't want this you have to let them know in good time. This can be a convenient way of operating for the customer because it cuts out the hassle of renewal, or looking for a better deal elsewhere. However, this system can actually tie you into a deal that no longer works on the same premium that you first took it out on, and the deal might not be as good as it was in the beginning. Check out any possible increases before you commit yourself. It is worth keeping up to date with insurance deals and be sure that you are getting the best one. Real savings can be made for those willing to take the time and effort to check these out. Prices can increase just a little each year so that you don't notice much of a change or you are at least willing to accept the small increase, yet over a period of time these can gradually increase significantly and so they are no longer such a good deal.

- Compare prices of insurance by visiting websites, here are some that could be helpful to you:
    - For car insurance: **comparethemarket.com**
    - For different types of insurance: **gocompare.com**

- Some people seek help from an insurance broker to get help in getting a deal that suits them.

Gifts

- Be a giver! With care, we should always be in a position to have something to give away. The Lord wants us to be able to give; we are actually the richer for giving.

- Making your own gifts can add a really personal touch to your present. People often appreciate the time and thought you have put into a gift you have made, far more than one that is bought. These are often remembered for years after they were given.

- Set an upper limit so that you keep within your budget and don't overspend!

- Don't feel guilty if you can't spend as much as you would like to; remember it's the thought that counts!

- If you can't spend money on a gift but you still want to give to that person, then maybe you could offer to do some chores for a person e.g. baby-sit, wash their car, clean their house, mow their lawn etc.

- Try to consider carefully what you give to a person; will they use the gift you have given? If not the money used is wasted.

- Unwanted gifts can be recycled and given to someone else, or even sold on e.bay; this could also be used to buy gifts.

- Also charity shops can make money from unwanted gifts; you can sow your gift!
- Many people use e.bay to buy and sell items and make money through this source.

Other Ideas

- Don't keep too much money in your purse or wallet then you won't be tempted to overspend. This helps to prevent you thinking you can have a spending spree when you really can't afford to. This also helps you to only buy things you really need or can afford.

- Try not to adopt the 'cheapo' mentality. It doesn't always work and you often end up paying twice with poor quality goods that break easily. Cheap is not always the best option in the long run.

- On-line banking can help you to keep a careful watch on what is going out and where to. Banks do make mistakes so check your account if your spending doesn't tally up with what the bank says. I once had £100 removed from my account by my bank by mistake!

- Do your budgeting weekly and keep your own record of all your outgoings and in. Keep an account of what you spend etc. with each of your savings accounts; include your direct debits as well. This way you can see at a glance just how much you have in your accounts. Keep this up to date and remember to write in all that you withdraw or deposit into each account. A simple way is to have just a few columns: date, details, (place of purchase/ or where money deposited has come from) amount deposited, amount withdrawn and finally the updated balance.

- Keep bank statements for a while in case you need to question something. Replacement statements often have to be paid for.

- Limit your shopping time to once a week. Try and do without things you run out of until your planned weekly shop. Calling in supermarkets for one or two things rarely happens; we often end up buying things we don't need while we are there.

- Many bargains can be found in pound shops, especially household items e.g. cleaning items, toilet rolls, washing up liquid, shampoo, etc.

- Consider doing a fast from spending, e.g. clothes fast! Don't buy any clothes for a few months and see how much you have saved. We can be challenged about our spending, are we materialistic? Do I really need another ....?

- Grow your own plants from seeds; seeds are a lot cheaper to buy than plants. This is also more satisfying and could provide you with lovely gifts to give e.g. hanging baskets, tubs of plants etc. Charity shops provide an interesting selection of containers which you could put plants in.

- Take in a lodger to help pay your bills; in some cases this could halve your utility bills in your home. This can also help to pay off your mortgage sooner rather than later. Remember though this will have to be declared and a single person would lose their single person entitlement off the council tax!

- Taking in overseas students every now and then can provide you with an extra income! This is a good solution if you want a lodger but don't want this situation permanently; they pay good rates for bed and breakfast lodging with a packed lunch and evening meal. The length of stay varies according to their circumstances, this can be short or longer term.

- Review budgeting and compare what you have spent in various areas so that you can see if you are unnecessarily overspending and you can bring change e.g. the phone bill.

- Keep a clock next to the phone and keep an eye on the time while you are using the phone! Time passes very quickly when you're having a good chat!

- Phone companies offer deals to reduce the size of your bill, e.g. free after 6 o'clock, calling named people etc. Look into these because they vary a lot. Also look into the deal that you get with your mobile phone you can get free texts and calls with some deals.

- Plant 'seeds' of money for specific things and water that seed by praying and confessing the relevant scriptures. This way you will encourage your faith to believe and receive!

Prayer of Salvation

Maybe you are reading or realising for the first time that the Lord Jesus truly cares for you; in fact He loves you with an unconditional love! He wants to bring you into a relationship with God the Father. Let's look at some scripture, all from the NIV.

First, we need to acknowledge that none of us are perfect.

Romans 3:23

> "for all have sinned and fall short of the glory of God"

Secondly, there are consequences for our sin.

Romans 6:23

> "For the wages of sin is death, but the gift of God is eternal life in Christ Jesus our Lord"

Thirdly, God responded to our situation long before we turned to Him, and He made provision for our salvation!

Romans 5:8

> "But God demonstrates his own love for us in this: While we were still sinners, Christ died for us.

Fourthly, nobody is excluded; all can be brought into a relationship with God the Father. We all have a choice!

Romans 10:13

> *"for, "Everyone who calls on the name of the Lord will be saved."*

This means whoever turns to the Lord can be saved! This is a personal invitation to you right now! You can receive salvation! No sin is too great to keep us from God!

If we ask God to forgive our sin He is faithful to His word.

1 John 1:9

> *"If we confess our sins, he is faithful and just and will forgive us our sins and purify us from all unrighteousness."*

How wonderful it is to have the slate wiped completely clean! Everything that we have done wrong in thought, word and deed is completely forgiven by God! We really can start again! Hallelujah!

If you would like to ask God to forgive all of your sin, and you would like to give your life to God, then please pray this prayer:

Dear Lord Jesus,

Please forgive me for all my sin; in thought, and word, and deed. I am truly sorry, and repent of all my sin. I ask you to forgive me and cleanse me and make me new. I receive your forgiveness and give my life to you! I am truly grateful for all that you have done! Thank you Jesus!

Amen

If you have prayed this prayer, and you really mean it, then you are now a son or daughter of the living God!

Start your walk with God by reading the Gospels of Matthew, Mark, Luke and John in the Bible.

Find a good bible believing church.

Start having fellowship with other believers.

Be blessed!

Lightning Source UK Ltd.
Milton Keynes UK
UKOW04f0156191115

263015UK00001B/6/P